HOW TO BUILD
AND GROW YOUR IT
CONSULTING STARTUP

Srikanth Merianda, BE, MS

DISCLAIMER

NOTE: If you are new to IT consulting, we highly recommend that you refer to our earlier book:

"How to Start and Run IT Consultancy Business: Become a Consultant, IT Entrepreneur or Start an Information Technology Consulting Firm"

https://www.amazon.com/How-Start-Run-Consultancy-Business-ebook/dp/B01J58E8PK/

Or,

Visit the following page for books on various sites.

https://www.consultingopportunity.com/books

ABOUT THE AUTHOR

Srikanth Merianda is a developer, entrepreneur, and investor with over 15 years of experience as employee and employer. He has worked for Convergys, Nortel Networks and Blackberry as Software Engineer, Project Manager, Architect, and Implementation of mission critical projects.

Srikanth has successfully started multiple IT Consulting Firms, Business process outsource Firms, and Mobile Apps development firms. He guided these companies through start-up, survival, turnaround and growth phases.

Besides setting up firms, Srikanth also provides IT consulting service to mission critical integration projects as well as technical and cost assessment for Software projects. With his wealth of experience, knowledge, and expertise, he has provided technical and business consulting services to companies and some have gone to gross over $1 million in their first year of getting consultancy services from him.

Srikanth is a passionate programmer and an enthusiastic learner of all things technology. He constantly looks for ways to make work and life easier with the tools provided by technology. He holds a Bachelors Engineering degree in Computer Science and a Master of Science in Computer Science from the Mississippi State University.

Contents

INTRODUCTION

Undoubtedly, being recognized as a small IT consulting startup is no easy task. It takes a lot of time and effort to get your business off the ground, and to keep it moving in the right direction - you just cannot expect your startup to become a huge success overnight! Why?

Because the battlefield is extremely tough, and competition even fiercer, which means you have work really hard before you can actually start seeing the traction you desire. Of course, this doesn't mean you need to start off by being under-confident or pessimistic.

On the contrary, be confident and positive in your abilities. Keep investing in yourself at every stage of your IT consulting startup, and try to grab the opportunities that come your way. While you may be tempted to push your message with interruptive marketing techniques, remember these are efforts people have learnt to ignore.

What exactly should you do then? Although it looks like a tough space to be successful in IT consulting for beginners, it's an easy job for someone who has been doing this as opportunities arise every day. In this eBook, you will find all the steps that you need to build and grow your IT consulting startup.

From creating a website to attract clients and effectively marketing your IT consulting business, to interacting with clients to get continuous job orders in your inbox and growing your IT consulting business, this eBook has all the advice to take your IT consulting startup to the next level. So, let's start the journey from startup to growth!

CHAPTER 1

CREATE AN IT CONSULTING WEBSITE THAT ATTRACTS CLIENTS

Are you taking full advantage of your brand presence online? Is your website built to establish you as an authority, and provide you with a healthy stream of leads to grow your business?

If you are like most IT consultants, it's likely that your website has room for improvement. So, without any further ado, let's look at how you can turn your website from being a source of information to a means for generating clients:

Step #1: Communicate Your USP

When a potential client visits your website, the first thing they should get to see is your unique selling point. Also common-ly referred to as a value proposition or competitive advantage, your USP is a short paragraph that instantly comprehends what you do, how you do it, who you do it for, and what makes YOU different than the rest of the competition.

Your unique selling point should be beamed at the visitor as soon as they land on your site. For instance, since you are selling IT consulting services, your USP should be something like: *Get the expert IT consulting you need for solving IT problems and streamlining business processes!*

The stronger your USP is, the more effective you will be in speaking to your potential clients. You will be able to convince them to go deeper into your website, and learn more about your company and the services you offer. And that, obviously, increases your chances of getting a new client.

Step #2: Design for the User

People on the internet do not read anymore, they scan! However, despite knowing this simple fact, many IT consulting websites are still designed based on what the owner thinks would look good and appealing - without even taking into account how people actually use websites.

Jakob Neilsen - renowned web usability expert - recommends making the text on your website scannable. This of course means you need to make the most crucial points stand out, the ones you actually want your site visitors to see. However, how do you go about this?

One effective way is to have certain text in **bold**, such as: ***Our IT consulting services are competitively priced!*** That drew your eye, didn't it? Using lists and bullets is another way. The whole idea behind this is to break up the text on your website to make it easier for visitors to scan through and quickly grasp the most important pieces of information.

For this reason, the font size you choose should be large enough so that your target audience can easily read it. Also, since visitors do not actually ready everything present on your website when they first arrive, clearly list what exactly you do and what services you offer!

Step #3: Show Them You Are Authentic

In the past few years, the online commerce industry has grown dramatically and this trend is expected to accelerate in the future. However, when it comes to shopping online, the main objection most people have is lack of trust, especially with the increase in cyber threats in recent times.

So, is your website providing your visitors with enough information for them to know you are whom you say you are? Have you placed a picture of yourself, or your team - i.e. if you have employees - on your website? If you are an independent IT consultant, showing your face is essential.

After all, in the consulting landscape, your main goal is to create relationships with potential clients and then solidify that relationship so they stay, and for that, showing yourself is the key! Therefore, you should provide enough information about your background and accomplishments to build credibility.

Not only this, you can also show testimonials from clients, logos of clients you have worked with, and anything else that would help to prove the point. You should do just about everything possible to dismiss any objection or hesitation the visitor may have in acquiring your services.

There are two other ways you can tackle this issue. First, you can provide a phone number to your office on your website. By doing so, people will be able to speak with you about any queries or concerns they have. Second, listing your physical address helps too as it shows you are accessible and have nothing to hide.

While things such as these may seem insignificant to you, the positive impact they have is significant!

Step #4: Color Does Matter

The colors you choose have a huge affect on website conversion. Hence, you need to be careful about which colors you decide to go with. There are two types of colors you should be aware about:

- **Action Colors** tell people to take a particular action. For instance, using orange or red buttons on your website clearly implies that visitors will be sent to another page when they click on them.

- **Passive Colors**, on the other hand, builds your brand image and identity. If your logo, or the color of your business cards is blue, you are better off incorporating blue throughout your website.

However, one of the most common mistakes IT consulting website owners make is that they mix both action and passive colors. For instance, if blue is their passive color, they will go with blue for their links as well. And with this, the problem only worsens if you have other text or a headline on the site that is blue, but not a link.

As a result, your visitors are likely to have a hard time figuring out what they should click, and what they should not. Therefore, it is important to be careful about using colors on your website.

Step #5: Forge Relationships

Let's take a closer look at what happens on most websites. A potential client visits your site - whether through a paid ad, online search or any other means - and tries to figure out what your IT consulting business has to offer, and if you could help them with a certain problem they are facing.

More often than not, they will either come back to your site later on or probably add it to their bookmarks (if you are lucky!).

When it comes to building relationships with potential clients, you have to admit this process does little to nothing! The more effective approach is to ask the visitor for their information.

It can be their name, email address or any other piece of information you require. Now, here is how your website works. A potential client visits your site and goes through the same process, but this time they will see that you are offering an email series, report or audio on a topic of their interest.

Think about it - wouldn't they enter their email address right away to take advantage of the offer? This way, even if they have left your website without making contact, you can follow up with them later on and offer them the valuable information, such as a newsletter or case study.

In fact, you can also notify them about a special offer or a new service you are going to introduce soon. Therefore, if you want to build relationships with your potential clients, this is the way to go about it!

Now that you have a better understanding of how you should create your IT consulting website to attract clients, let's move on to the next chapter where we will discuss a number of effective ways you can market your IT consulting business to the masses.

You can use this as a benchmark and expand on your niche skill in IT consulting. However, if you need to use some templates and content to get started, you can visit our website for using services from outsource firms for a flat fee. Visit www.consultin-gooportunity.com/quickstart and select the service you need to get some quotes as an alternative to your efforts.

CHAPTER 2

WAYS TO EFFECTIVELY MARKET YOUR IT CONSULTING BUSINESS

So, you want to get more clients for your IT consulting business? While there are a number of ways you can go about this, you first need to take some time to work out who is your ideal consulting client. After all, how can your market to them if you have no idea who they actually are!

To get you started, we would refer you to one of our own clients who can provide you Job Orders or Resources for your Job orders (a.k.a source candidates). Please go to <u>www.consultingopportunity.com/lead</u> and fill-up the information about your firm to be forewarned to ONE vendor firm for free. This should get you started on at-least 10 orders per week if you are looking to work on contract positions to be filled up.

Identifying Your Ideal Client

Who exactly is your ideal consulting client? What type of clients you want to market your business to? At this stage of your IT consulting startup, it is important that you work out the criteria to determine your ideal client. An easy way to do this is by listing the traits of people you would like to work with.

Once you have managed to do this properly, you will be able to effectively drive the marketing process forward and gain exposure to your ideal clients. Therefore, make sure you take your time and do not rush through this part, otherwise you will lack clarity on who your ideal client is.

Since all of your marketing efforts - your unique selling point and marketing message strategy - will be based on this, it is critical that you have your REAL client in sight.

The More Focused You Are, the Better

To attract more clients, you need to be focused. As a matter of fact, the more focused you are on who your ideal consulting client is, the better the chances that they will find you during their search.

You will be able to figure out who your ideal client is, where they are located, and what their title is, allowing you to target your marketing and messaging directly towards them. However, many IT consultants find themselves reluctant to narrow down and focus on their ideal client.

Now, why is that so? Well, this process can be hard for consultants because they feel it is restrictive to narrow on a specific client. They think that they will end up losing many opportunities if their focus is on a specific client type. Sure, it is a big shift to make in your mindset, but it is a crucial one!

Look at any successful IT consulting company out here, and you will find that they have a clear focus on their target market early on. It's how they have built their brand name, and established themselves as experts in their field. That is exactly what you need to do as well.

For example, if you can find resources to fit jobs that are based on Java, you can also start focusing on a BPM tools such as Pega as they are closely related by Java Programming. This would let you approach clients for projects as well once you have your own list of consultants working on various customer locations.

Finding Your Consulting Clients

Once you are absolutely clear on who your ideal consulting client is, and you have narrowed down your focus to the right client, now it's time you get to work on finding them.

When it comes to marketing your startup, it is not about choosing the most popular strategy or method. Yes, just because one type of marketing is working out well for someone, it does not necessarily mean it would for you too!

Think about it - if the same marketing method worked perfectly for every business, would not there only be one marketing method? Surely, you get the point! Therefore, before you decide what marketing method you are going to choose, you need to ask yourself a number of questions:

- Where are my ideal consulting clients?

- Where can I get my message in front of them?

- What websites and blogs do they visit?

- What groups or associations they are a part of?

- What events do they attend?

- What publications do they read?

These are just some of the many questions that can help you in finding your ideal consulting clients and getting you in front of them, so that you can put your message forward.

For example, if the client is using an application or software to run a process or business and this project needs programmers specialized in Java, you can pitch them with PEGA which is an automation tool for Java Programming. There are many tools that help businesses implement their process in terms of rules and make their business process more automated and steamlined

5 Methods to Get Consulting Clients

There are countless ways available to promote your IT consulting services to your ideal clients. Below we have listed and discussed 5 of the most effective methods that you can use, but keep in mind that the one(s) you choose will be primarily dependent on who exactly your ideal client is and where you can efficiently and effectively reach them:

Small Events

A great way to attract more consulting clients is by hosting small events. You should invite a particular number of potential buyers to the event, conduct a short, informational presentation, and then facilitate a discussion. These events provide a great opportunity to communicate and demonstrate the value your business can deliver.

Unlike webinars, you can meet the attendees face-to-face, shake hands, and have meaningful conversations with them to build trust and establish your credibility around your brand or services. While physically organizing events such as these can involve a lot of legwork, they are not that hard to do and the return on invest can be huge as well!

Paid Advertising

Most IT consulting startups do not think about advertising, mainly because they feel they cannot afford it and the results are not usually impressive. However, paid advertising - if used the right way - can prove extremely effective in generating leads and attract consulting clients.

Facebook Ads - which allows you to target specific groups of people - is a powerful way to attract leads for certain markets. LinkedIn Ads, on the other hand, is great option for other markets. Google Adwords, though, remains the most popular ad platform used by many marketers across the world. In the end, it all comes down to determining which platform can help you reach your ideal clients.

Whichever platform you decide to go with, it is important to be careful when deciding on how much money to spend on advertising. If you have no idea what you are doing, you can end up spending a lot of money on ads, that too, without making any considerable impact!

It is crucial that you approach your paid advertising campaign strategically from the start, so that you can quickly attract clients, convert leads into profit, and then scale your IT consulting business from up there. If you want to learn more about using advertising to attract more consulting clients, visit my website to gain all the knowledge and training you need: www.consultingopportunity.com.

Direct Mail

This is one of the best - not to mention cheapest - ways to drum up new business as it is targeted to exactly the clients you want to reach. All you have to do is rent or create a targeted prospect list, and then send your potential clients a sales letter, flier or brochure describing the range of IT consulting services your business offer, with a gift enclosed.

You have to be careful when crafting the wording for each interaction, because this process will allow you to identify your ideal consulting clients, engage them, and ultimately speak or meet with them to have a sales conversation. Don't know how you should go about this? Here are some tips that will help you create attention-grabbing direct mail:

- **Place a compelling message outside the envelope.** Words such as "Limited time offer", "Competitive prices" and "Free" are all great attention-grabbers that can convince the recipient of your mail to open the envelope and see what is being offered.

- **Highlight the benefits of your services, and give all the related details in the sales letter.** Then you should make it easy to respond or request additional information easy. For this, give your website URL, phone number and email address. Include a postage-paid envelope or postcard as well, so that if they are interested it is not impossible to get back to you!

- **Personalize your message.** By using a mail merge program, you can address the recipient by their name on each envelope. Similarly, the sales letter inside the envelope must be directed to that particular recipient by name.

Research Leads in LinkedIn

LinkedIn is not just a tool to connect with other professionals, and can be used to deliver the context you need to provide uniquely customized solutions and answer difficult questions. In short, it also helps you in getting to know your leads - even before you actually call or meet them!

By reviewing the profiles of your leads, you can get a better idea of whom you are speaking with. So, search them up on LinkedIn, and go through their profile to get a general understanding of what they do. After all, you should be able to relate to the people you are talking to in order to make an effective outreach.

Take a close look at their work experience, qualifications and certifications, as well as the news, groups and companies they are following to better understand how you can influence the sale. You will inevitable gain a lot of information about your leads by searching on LinkedIn.

However, the upside is not just having that information, but also using it in a way to create a context for your call or meeting. Also, make sure to use ancillary items like their current position, job role and length of employment to understand where their interests presently lie.

Email & Call the Leads

Once you have gathered enough information about your leads, it is time to email and call them. These are the most direct ways to get in front of your ideal clients consistently, and create the opportunities you need to have conversations that will ultimately lead to more business.

However, it is important to have the right mindset when calling and emailing your leads. Rather than cold-calling and spamming people, realize that it is a great way to build a relationship with them. So, use the information you found on LinkedIn, and ask right questions during your sales conversation.

Position yourself well enough to effectively communicate your value to your ideal client. Diagnose the problem they are facing, and if it is a good fit, offer them the right solution. Since you will already know a little about your leads, you will feel more confident and that is exactly what will help you land more job orders at high fee levels.

To make things easier for you, we are offering you 100 email leads free of cost. All you have to do is visit <u>www.consultingopportunity.com</u> and sign up to our newsletter.

With all that out of the way, let us move on to the next chapter where you will learn how to interact with your clients to get job orders more consistently!

CHAPTER 3

INTERACTING WITH CLIENTS FOR JOB ORDERS

You need to set up the infrastructure and communication platform of your IT consulting business before you can start taking job orders from clients. Job orders will be coming in every day with several other IT consulting companies delivering their resumes and sales pitches via email or social media in order to get these organizations to work with them.

Things You Will Need

- An email address - such as hotmail or Gmail - that would be able to hold large amounts of email, and offer search capabilities.

- Resumes for submitting to these jobs.

- Google Docs or Excel to keep track of your submission list to follow up.

- Non-Compete Agreement to protect your business' customers, trade secrets and innovations.

- Direct Client Requirements from vendors who have clients that need professionals to come in and work on their projects.

- 3rd Party requirements from Tier 1 or Tier 2 vendors that you do not have access to.

Process to Fill the Job Order

- Screen the job orders that come into your email inbox, and determine which ones you want to work on.

- Find a matching resume for the job that's quick or hard to fill.

- Format the resume in a neat and professional manner.

- Rate Non-Compete Agreement and confirmation signed by the employer.

- Use the submission form to send the resume.

- Move on to the next job.

Qualifying the Job Order

If you are thinking that claims of "being different' or promises to "build relationships" will wow your potential clients, think again! You need to do much more than that to impress them, and qualify for the job order. But how? Here's what you need to keep in mind:

- **Don't Over Promise:** If you think you don't have the capabilities to get the job done, just say so! Honesty is the best policy and the same goes when it comes to your clients. The next time around, they will probably come back to you with job orders you can actually handle.

- **Explain What Actually Separates You From the Rest:** You should be able to tell your potential clients within 15 to 20 seconds what makes you the best choice, that too without delivering the typical sales pitch they have probably heard a million times.

- **Provide One Point-of-Contact:** Your clients are likely to prefer dealing with the same person every time they have a job order that needs to be completed. Therefore, if your IT consulting business has retention issues, they need to be taken care of immediately!

If you need any templates for NCA or Contract or Agreement, you can visit our website www.consultingoportunity.com/resoures. While most resources we have are free, some are paid with minimal fee to cover the cost of delivery. You can use these as templates, customize them accordingly, and approach any attorneys to review them online or locally to make sure the rules and regulations comply to the state you reside in.

CHAPTER 4

HOW TO GROW YOUR IT CONSULTING BUSINESS

Once you have achieved some success in marketing your IT consulting business, landed a client or two, and successfully completed their projects on time and within budget, you need to focus on developing a loyal customer base and growing your business further.

The question here is how you go about it. Growing your IT consulting business will undoubtedly require a lot of time and effort. It can be painful trying to scale your ability to take on more projects in a profitable and productive way. However, things can be made less challenging by moving in the right direction, so here's what you need to keep in mind:

Get Continuous Job Orders from Current Clients

If you have exerted a great deal of effort to get your first clients - well, you are not alone! Over the years, there have been several studies that attest to the effort involved in client acquisition. Bain & Company - one of the world's leading management consulting firms - reports it can cost 6 to 7 times more to acquire a new customer than to retain an existing one. Also, let's not forget the time involved as both go-hand-in-hand.

For this reason, it's extremely important you stay on the lookout for opportunities to get additional work from your existing clientele. So, keep your eyes and ears open while you work on projects and document the opportunities you notice, including your proposed approach or solution. Then, when your client sees the quality work you have delivered and you are close to wrapping up the project, discuss the opportunities you came across.

Chances are they might know some of them, and not be fully aware about the others. However, don't feel discouraged if the client doesn't move forward with your proposals right away. If nothing else, at least your dedication and effort will be appreciated, and that's essential for keeping your clients coming back to your IT consulting business. Therefore, stay in touch with them and continue to look for opportunities to get more job orders.

Focus on the clients that can close deals in the beginning than the ones which are trial and error. This will help you generate some revenue and understand the process as you proceed. Once you know how to work with one client, try to automate or outsource as much you can.

Although we have some resources on our website about out-house we will be coming up with a book about outsourcing tasks to run IT consulting business with minimal expense soon. If you have subscribed to our newsletter you would get a notification when the book is made available.

You will be receiving some free content - books or audio books as much as we can give away. So, if you haven't subscribed to our newsletter already, now would be a good time to subscribe to do it.

Network with Other IT Consultants

One of the main reasons why organizations opt for larger firms - as opposed to small and medium companies - is their ability to maintain a wide variety of consultants on its roster to develop a complete solution for client needs. Does that mean your IT consulting business is out of the picture? Not really. You can actually provide the same level and quality of service to your clients as well.

All you have to do is network with other IT consultants who are capable of engaging in projects of varying nature. For instance, instead of just recommending to your client that he/she needs to adopt a human resource management system, you should offer to develop a custom- tailored solution for them. If you don't have the required technical know-how, though, simply partner with another IT consultant that does!

These alliances can prove mutually beneficial as they provide you with new opportunities as well. However, don't partner with just anybody - you should be absolutely comfortable with the quality of work they deliver. After all, if one of your existing clients is not satisfied, this would reflect poorly on your budding IT consulting business.

Revaluate Your Niche

As you continue to work on projects and identify opportunities to get additional job orders, reevaluate your skills and how you market your IT consulting business. You will realize that you are learning new skills and knowledge in the course of your work, giving you the capability to deliver a wider range of services to your clients.

So, when working on your clients' project, think about how it could be applied in a completely different situation, or how you can develop a solution set to market to other organizations. You need to make sure all your marketing materials - like business cards, brochures, emails and ads - are updated accordingly to reflect these changes.

Treat Your References as Gold & Gain Additional Leads

As you establish yourself in the IT consulting market, new clients will ask for references of similar jobs you have done in the recent past in order to evaluate your skills and eligibility. However, it's important to note that checking previous client references is usually a far more thorough process as opposed to that performed for a job application or resume.

The client makes calls to request details of the job, and more importantly, inquire about your specific performance. Remember, you must have the permission of your client to use them as a reference! Make sure to let them know that you have included them in a job proposal, and that they may be contacted. But don't - **we repeat don't** - overuse them!

After all, they are not running a business only to field questions about your performance or skills. While this can prove a little difficult at first, especially when your experience is limited, you will be able to spread your references around as you gain more experience. This way, the same clients would not always be contacted, and that's a win-win for everyone.

Protect Yourself

Once your IT consulting business is established and running well - with employees handling a majority of the responsibilities on a daily basis - you should consider meeting with a professional attorney to discuss the legal options you have available to protect yourself.

The assets you have worked day and night to accumulate may be lost in a short period of time if they are not protected. There are a number of specific acts passed by lawmakers, like Professional Corporation and Limited Liability Corporation, which can help you protect your personal assets.

You should also learn about professional liability insurance and other relevant products from a business insurance provider. In the past, there have been several instances of litigation where consultants from various fields have been sued for damages far beyond their reach.

Organizations have held consultants responsible for increased expenses and lost revenue due to failed implementation. Settlements such as these can not only wipe out a small startup, but also cause personal damage to the consultant if their assets are not protected.

CONCLUSION

And that's about it! With that, you have reached the conclusion of the eBook, "How to Build and Grow Your IT Consulting Startup". If you want to take your IT consulting startup to new heights, but don't quite know where and how you should get started, follow the steps mentioned in this eBook, and rest assured you will achieve the success you long for!

BONUS:

As a bonus to our valued readers, we will be adding each one of you to a vendor company that has both Tier-1 and Direct Client vendor jobs! All you have to do is sign up to our newsletter at ConsultingOpportunity.com, and you are good to go.

NOTE: If you are new to IT consulting, we highly recommend that you refer to our earlier book:

"How to Start and Run IT Consultancy Business: Become a Consultant, IT Entrepreneur or Start an Information Technology Consulting Firm"

https://www.amazon.com/How-Start-Run-Consultancy-Business-ebook/dp/B01J58E8PK/

Or,

Visit the following page for books on various sites.

https://www.consultingopportunity.com/books

TERMINOLOGIES

USP

The unique selling point is the standout factor which distinguishes a product or service from the competition.

IT

Information technology refers to the systems which are used for communicating information.

PEGA

PEGA is a tool developed for facilitating management of different business processes.

URL

A uniform resource locator is the online address for a website.

Tier 1 & Tier 2

An unofficial ranking based on the market share and reputation of different vendors

Non-Compete Agreement

A non-compete agreement outlines that a vendor will not enter into competition with another